ONE HUNDRED WAYS

ONE HUNDRED WAYS

A HANDBOOK FOR WRITING 100-WORD STORIES

RAN WALKER

BLACK AND SQUARE PAPERBACK EDITION

Cover photo courtesy of Eugenio Mazzone
Cover Design by Randolph Walker, Jr.
Illustrations courtesy of Zulfan Muhammad

ISBN: 978-1-961753-10-5 (Paperback)
ISBN: 978-1-961753-11-2 (Ebook)

First Edition
10 9 8 7 6 5 4 3 2

Black and Square
An Imprint of 45 Alternate Press, LLC
Hampton Roads, VA

CONTENTS

For Elle and Zoë

PREFACE

Why write a book about writing 100-Word stories?

After writing over 1,000 100-word stories, I decided to put together my top 100 tips into one place, should writers need support, encouragement, or just information on how to write a better and stronger 100-word story.

Because each of the chapters that follow contain exactly 100 words each, I did not want to use space for story examples when there are plenty of them on the Internet. I have, however, included a bibliography if you are seeking a more curated list of books composed of 100-word stories.

Good luck and happy writing!

"Don't tell me the moon is shining; show me the glint of light on broken glass."

— ANTON CHEKHOV

PART I

UNDERSTANDING THE 100-WORD STORY

1

WHAT IS A 100-WORD STORY?

A 100-word story is a story in which the entirety of it is expressed in exactly 100 words. This does not include the title, which, if you were inclined, could be used to expand your story slightly, should you choose to make your title the first line of the story.

This type of story, oftentimes referred to as a "drabble," must have a beginning, middle, and ending, though not necessarily in that order, and many of those elements are usually implied to the reader, as opposed to appearing directly on the page.

100-word stories fall under the sub-genre of microfiction.

2

WHAT IS MICROFICTION?

Microfiction is one of the smallest storytelling forms available to writers. Different from both short stories and flash fiction, microfiction is typically defined as stories consisting of 500 words or fewer, with most literary journals, anthologies, and competitions preferring 300 words or fewer.

Under the umbrella of microfiction are 100-word stories, 50-word stories, and even six-word stories. With lengths that range from one typed page to a single line of text, microfiction must be approached differently than short stories and flash fiction. We will discuss some of the strategies for writing these kinds of stories in the subsequent chapters.

3

HOW DOES THE 100-WORD STORY DIFFER FROM FLASH FICTION?

Because the word count is, by default, shorter than flash fiction (let alone short stories), 100-word stories must be approached from the standpoint of both greater brevity and greater focus. What would typically be done in three or four pages must now be done in a paragraph or, at least, half of a single page. That leaves little room for setting up stories with more traditional plot structures and instead requires you to begin the story much closer to the climax—and possibly right after it. Even more, 100-word stories have fixed word counts, further refining the scope of storytelling.

4

MAKING THE DECISION TO WRITE
100-WORD STORIES

Writing a story using 100 words can be daunting on the surface. Most of the stories you have read likely have far more words, far more details, and far more going on, in general. In fact, many writers are content to simply question how a person could possibly write one and never venture to try one themselves.

The level of focus on story (and what can be implied), as well as language choices, diction, grammar, and mechanics, provide plenty of practice for good, sound writing.

Writing in this form can provide discipline to any writing routine, whether long or short.

5

DRIBBLES AND DRABBLES AND TERMINOLOGY

The most common of the microfiction stories that contain fixed word counts are dribbles and drabbles.

While the words sound funny, they are commonly used to refer to stories of 50 words and stories of 100 words, respectively.

If you thought 100-word stories were challenging to write, then the idea of a 50-word story must be far more daunting. Ironically, though, I first developed my skills for writing 100-word stories by first writing more than a hundred 50-word stories.

As we will cover later on, sometimes starting short and building up can be the best approach to writing these stories.

6

UNDERSTANDING WHAT A 100-WORD STORY IS

S tories are like plants that grow to the size of their pots. If the pot is small, the plant will be small. If the pot is large, the plant will be large. The same idea that could fuel a 100-word story could also fuel a full-length novel.

If you know you're writing the "drabble" version of the story, you will likely spend much of your time figuring out and isolating the most significant part of the story to put on display. It's like looking at a painting and focusing on the most interesting part— then writing your story around it.

7

UNDERSTANDING WHAT A 100-WORD STORY IS NOT

While a 100-word story can be many things, one thing it cannot be is a novel. It will never inhabit the depth and breath of an extended work of fiction, and to this end, there is little point in trying to tell a large, complex story in a small space. The only way to come remotely close to this is to summarize the idea, and summaries are not stories.

You'll want to lock in on the most resonant part of your story and use that as the focus of your story.

It's not a miniature version; it's its own story.

8

READ AS MANY 100-WORD STORIES AS YOU CAN

Just as a poet should read poetry or a playwright should read plays, a microfictionist should reach the work of other microfictionists.

One of the benefits that comes from doing this is that it can show you numerous ways in which an author can craft a story in such a limited space. You can examine techniques, writing styles, the use of language, how plot is written (or implied), how character is developed (or implied), as well as various experimental approaches that would only work with microfiction and, more specifically, drabbles.

Reading the work of others is as important as writing.

WHERE TO FIND 100-WORD STORIES

There was a time when you had to hunt to find 100-word stories. Thankfully, that is no longer the case.

Since Paul Strohm and Grant Faulkner first published their respective collections of drabbles, a number of literary journals (most of them online) have emerged, providing microfictionists plenty of places to submit their stories. I have identified several of these journals by name in Chapter 82 farther along in this book.

There are likely to be more journals popping up as the form grows in popularity and people find themselves either wanting to write or read more of these tiny gems.

10

GIVING YOURSELF PERMISSION
TO TRY SOMETHING NEW

If you have been writing for a while now and you feel yourself getting mired in the writing of a novel (or even a short story), writing a 100-word story might help you to get a reprieve and offer you the opportunity to redirect your creative energies into something with a more immediate return on time, energy, and investment. This is not to say writing a drabble is *easy*, but it should, in theory, require less energy that writing a novel.

Give yourself permission to see things through a different lens, to think about your ideas in a different way.

PART II

FINDING IDEAS

11

CREATE A FOLDER ON YOUR DIGITAL DEVICE TO COLLECT IDEAS

After having written over 1,000 drabbles, I learned that you have to always have ideas on the ready. In theory, a number of these ideas could be the seeds for novels, but instead I have chosen to write them in 100 words. That means you have to train yourself to be an idea factory.

Create a folder on your digital device to catch ideas as they come. Don't discriminate. Don't try to write the story. Just record the idea.

This is your personal list of ideas. You will draw from these ideas on days when your creative well is empty.

12

CONSIDER USING A POCKET NOTEBOOK

I use Field Notes memo books to write down ideas when they arise. When I journal, ideas will usually come to me. I have discovered that writing things down on paper forces my brain to work in a different way than it would if I were sitting at a computer. This intimate act of bringing the tip of a pen or pencil across a blank sheet of paper holds within it some type of inexplicable alchemy for writing. It also helps me to feel connected to writers of earlier generations. That feeling can oftentimes serve as inspiration for my writing.

13

ALWAYS ASK "WHY?"

This is the question at the heart of all fiction, regardless of genre. As you kick around ideas, gradually incorporate "why" into your process.

Why is the story starting here?

Why is this the best character for telling this story?

Why am I opening with this sentence?

Always be willing to interrogate your writing. Answering "just because" is never a good reason.

Even though you are showing a sliver of something and implying what surrounds it, that does not preclude you from knowing the "why" of your choices. You must know the full iceberg, even if you don't show it.

14

READ THE NEWS

S ome of the best ideas for microfiction come from reading the news. The apocryphal story "For sale: baby shoes, never worn," commonly attributed to Ernest Hemingway, had its origins in a newspaper. In fact, the first novel I ever wrote was inspired by an article I read in the *New York Times*.

The key to writing about things from the news is that you should lean towards fictionalizing what you write to avoid potential legal issues. Create your own characters and motivations. Figure out the most interesting parts of those stories and add them to your desktop folder or notebook.

15

COLLECT YOUR DREAMS

I cannot begin to tell you the number of stories I have written that were inspired by dreams. I used to have dreams that were so vivid I knew I would certainly remember them when I sat down to write them. In the end, I forgot over 90% of them, and when I went to write down the remaining 10%, the magic of the idea had worn off, my mind having sobered too much to appreciate it.

Now I keep my notebook and phone next to my bed, ready to write down my dreams as soon as I wake up.

16

PAY ATTENTION TO YOUR SURROUNDINGS

Interestingly, the most story-worthy things to write about are around us, if only we pay attention to them. For example, if you're standing in line somewhere, take a look at what is going on in the area. Try to imagine what the people in line were doing before they got there and what they will do when they leave. Ask the question "what if?" The best stories understand something fundamental about human nature. This alone makes paying attention to your surroundings a necessity. It also provides plenty of possibilities for story ideas.

The next time you go out, take notes.

17

FIND INSPIRATION IN MUSIC

Music has become so integral to my writing process that I sometimes compile playlists to listen to as I write. Music evokes ideas. Because music is so heavily intertwined with films and story-telling, we have conditioned ourselves to visualize things in response to the music we hear.

I listen to a lot of instrumental jazz when I write. It gives my mind the opportunity to percolate ideas with arpeggios and laze about with legatos.

Music helps you to better visualize scenes, to inhabit moments—and when you are writing a drabble, there is nothing more important than inhabiting a scene.

18

WATCH MOVIES

Movies are essentially a collection of scenes that have been arranged to tell an impactful story. As microfictionists, we must examine those scenes, determine their relevance, understand what makes a scene breathe. Oftentimes a 100-word story is a scene in which something changes. The change doesn't have to be dramatic, but it has to be there: a realization, a choice, a decisive action, a decisive inaction.

This does not mean a 100-word story is simply a scene (after all there are thousands of different ways o write them), but it does mean that close examination of a moment is important.

WRITE DOWN THINGS YOU FIND INTERESTING

Have you ever been somewhere and heard a random fact that blew your mind?

Polar bears are really black (their hair is translucent, not white).

Purple is not a real color.

There are more identified cryptids than you'd believe.

Anytime I hear something unusual, something that flies in the face of my current thinking, it causes me to pause and reexamine what I think I know. This is great for creativity.

Jot those things down in your notebook or on your computer. You might find a way to use them later. At minimum, they will keep you on your toes.

20

USE A DICTIONARY

One of the easiest ways to get ideas for writing drabbles is to open the dictionary and flip to a random word. With that word, you could incorporate it into a story or write a word inspired by that definition.

What I love most are words I have never heard before, whether they be archaic or neologistic or just simply words that were beyond my current radar. Sometimes I will use the word as the title of the story, then write a story that feels like an example of the word being used in a sentence.

The options are endless.

PART III

WRITING YOUR FIRST 100-WORD STORY

DISPEL THE NOTION THAT IT IS IMPOSSIBLE TO WRITE A STORY IN 100 WORDS

The most common comment I have received from people when they find out I write 100-word stories is this: "I just don't see how you can write a story in 100 words." Some have even added they see 100 words as a paragraph and they have written full pages before anything significant has happened.

I understand this. I have been there.

The thing to keep in mind is all parts of a plot do not have to be on the page, only what is necessary. Remember this: you, the writer, are entering into a metaphorical, symbiotic relationship with your reader.

FIRST APPROACH TO WRITING
100-WORD STORIES

The most common approach to writing 100-word stories is taking a longer story and cutting out words until you get down to 100 words. I would caution against this approach.

My first attempt at a 100-word story was trimming out 650 words of a 750-word story. By the time I had finished, it looked like I had cut out—you guessed it—650 words that probably should have remained.

I analogize this with a person getting too much cosmetic plastic surgery. The story should be recognizable, even after the edits.

Remember the story should feel complete at its final length.

SECOND APPROACH TO WRITING 100-WORD STORIES

The second approach is to build up from a shorter story.

I can hear you saying, "How could I build up when the 100-word story is kicking my behind already?"

Relinquish what you think of as a short story and look at a story of fewer than 10 words, like the apocryphal aforementioned Hemingway story or Augusto Monterroso's "The Dinosaur." Smith College also has a plethora of six-word stories available to read. If you can learn to communicate at incredibly short lengths, writing 100 words is more than enough to flesh out an idea.

I prefer to use this method.

24

BE WILLING TO EXAMINE MORE CLOSELY WHAT YOUR STORY IDEA IS

Oftentimes when we come up with ideas for stories, those ideas might play out like miniature films in our heads. We then become married to every piece of the story arc and see each piece as indispensable. If we were to look a little closer, though, we might notice that much of what we are writing is to build up to something interesting happening. When this happens, we can convince ourselves that the "interesting" thing is the important thing.

I beg to differ.

The most important thing is how our characters react to that interesting thing, not the thing itself.

CUT TO THE CHASE

Now that we know it's about the character's response to that "interesting" thing, we can eliminate anything that does not specifically serve that purpose or that moment.

Trust me. I understand that you have so many really cool things you envisioned, but every detail is not relevant to the focus of your drabble. With so few words, you have to get into the story quickly. I'm not saying you have to begin in medias res, but you should probably start close to where you plan to end up.

It's like shooting a short film. Shrink the world to your form.

26

NEVER LOSE SITE OF THE KEY
MOMENT IN A SCENE

Once we are focused on the "interesting" thing, we have to hold it tenderly. We can't rush past it in pursuit of something even more interesting. We also can't treat it as one of several interesting things along the way. In short, it is important to really know what your story is about.

This is not always clear at first. Sometimes you have to discus your story with others to see what theme emerges. When you are more aware of your story and what it is you truly want to say, you can lock in on telling the best version.

27

DON'T WRITE WHAT CAN BE IMPLIED

Unless your story is about your character sleeping, we don't need to see that character wake up, brush her teeth, get dressed, or eat breakfast. We don't need to see a character opening a door. We don't even need to see the teacher handing out that "F" essay to a student. All of those things can be implied simply by starting the story in the right place. If the kid has a mask pushed up to his forehead and is sitting on the couch digging through a bucket of candy, we already know he just returned from trick or treating.

USE AN ENGAGING FIRST SENTENCE

Although 100 words is not a lot, we cannot take for granted that a reader will read the entire thing. If you doubt this, consider how people will scroll through an endless list of TikTok videos.

To that end, you have to engage the reader with the first sentence. Write something interesting, not explosive. You want your story to build, not hit the reader with a sentence the rest of your story could never live up to.

Your readers should want to read the next sentence or the next line. If you organize the story properly, they will read everything.

29

MAKE SURE YOUR ENDING RESONATES

I deally, the last sentence should linger on after the story has finished. I hesitate to say that you would want to leave your reader wanting more, mainly because that could be taken two ways: it was too good to end or, on the converse, it felt incomplete.

Because drabbles require cooperation from the imagination of your reader, you want her so invested in the story it feels like it is now with her, inhabiting the same space, expanding in her consciousness like a blossoming flower.

To make a resonate ending, you should understand the best place to end your story.

30

DON'T WORRY IF YOUR FIRST
STORY ISN'T VERY GOOD

Hemingway said it best about first drafts. Anne Lamott echoed it in her book *Bird by Bird*. And they are right: first drafts are usually crap. Accept that and get over it.

Writing is not an equation of The Universe to the brain to the pen to the page, with everything being sacred. Writing is work. It is trial and error, rewriting, editing, even debating commas and word choices. It's messy, but a good kind of messy.

Understand that the story in your head and the one on the page will never be the same—and that is all right.

PART IV

UNDERSTANDING PLOT

THE HERO'S JOURNEY AND WHY IT DOESN'T WORK FOR 100-WORD STORIES

The hero's journey typically involves a character who has been called to go on a quest. The character will confront a series of obstacles and eventually return home a changed individual. This is ideal for many stories, but for microfiction, it doesn't work. Trying to cram a story with this plot structure into 100 words is asking for the kind of headache from which nothing good could possibly come.

This isn't to say you can't have a quest or obstacles or a changed character; you simply can't have all of these things in the same story without over-compressing your story.

FREYTAG'S PYRAMID AND WHY IT DOESN'T WORK EITHER

Freytag's pyramid is composed of five elements: exposition, rising action, climax, falling action, and denouement. This is one of the most popular plot structures throughout storytelling, and just like the hero's journey, it doesn't work well with 100-word stories.

The problem, again, is that there are too many components to cover in the span of 100 words. You can, however, start at certain points along this pyramid and imply the rest. In fact, it might be easier to draw from this structure, even if you can't use the full pyramid. The key lies with understanding how to use the climax.

THINKING ABOUT THE CLIMAX

The climax is the highest point of tension in a story. In many cases, it is the point at which the protagonist has to make a decision that has major repercussions. Many novice short story writers like to end their stories on a cliff, a surprise ending, if you will. While there is nothing inherently wrong with doing this, it is rather cliché in the 21st century.

Instead of ending on the climax, consider starting your story immediately after the climax. How your protagonist responds to the climax is more interesting than the climax itself, so lean more into that.

34

KNOWING EXACTLY WHERE TO START

S tarting after the climax is a solid place to start (for reasons mentioned in the previous chapter). However, you are free to start your story in any location that will draw in the attention of the reader.

To do this effectively, it is important to understand all facets of the story as you envision them. Once you know every part of the story, it is important to be honest with yourself and home in on the moment in the story that hooks your reader and allows for your backstory to be implied in a way that moves the story forward.

PICK A SCENE THAT TELLS A STORY

Sometimes simply picking the right scene will reveal everything you need to know about the story. If your story opens with your protagonist sitting down to a two-person table and there is only silverware and plating on one side, you have illustrated a loneliness in the character. Adding a detail or two transforms this character into a widow. Now ask yourself, "Why am I showing this widow eating alone?" If loneliness is your selected theme, maybe you could conclude the story with a knock on the door from an unexpected individual, someone who might help to break our protagonist's loneliness.

36

THINK LIKE A FILMMAKER

A film is a collection of scenes that, once arranged in a particular order, tell a story. Sometimes you will find films where the scenes have "beats," which feel like smaller moments that could easily be self-contained. Writing a novel can be like that, but microfiction is *definitely* like that.

Think about the scene that will mean the most to your story. That will be the scene you write. If you approach that scene from the right angle, you can imply all of the relevant things that came before it and imply all of the things that surround that moment.

37

THINK LIKE A POET

One of the luxuries you have when working on a 100-word story is that you get to deep dive into language. With 100 words, every single word matters, just as if you were a poet.

Consider using various poetic devices to help enrich and enliven your writing, devices such as alliteration, assonance, metaphor, imagery, personification, onomatopoeia, homophones/homonyms/homographs, and a boatload of other techniques.

There is already a thin line between microfiction and prose poetry, so why not explore that ambiguity in your writing. A narrative prose poem and a poetic microfiction piece could be published in either genre.

38

IMPLYING THINGS TO YOUR READER

While we have touched on using implication in your writing, I would be remiss if I didn't qualify this further with an example.

Take a work of art like Jean-Michel Basquiat's *Pegasus*, Hieronymus Bosch's *The Garden of Earthly Delights*, Jackson Pollock's *Convergence*, or even a *Where Is Waldo?* poster. Pick the most interesting area within the artwork. Your goal is to write about that area of the artwork in such a way that the reader can envision the parts of the painting you are not showing.

It's like shining a flashlight around a dark room and focusing your gaze.

EVERY STORY BEGINS AND ENDS SOMEWHERE

Before Dorothy and Toto got blown away into Oz, there were things of interest that were happening in her life. After she returned from Oz, there were interesting things about her life that continued to occur. We don't get to see those things, though. We only get to see what L. Frank Baum elected to show us. Every story is like that.

Because you can start a story anywhere and end a story anywhere, what you decide to show will be the story you write.

With microfiction, the narrower the story you want to tell, the better off you'll be.

40

BE PREPARED TO REVISE UNTIL YOU GET IT RIGHT

Your first draft might be 125 words, or it might be 75 words. This is okay. You have to get the story down before you can begin to revise it. At this point, nothing is sacred, so focus on getting the idea down indiscriminately. Editing a blank page is next to impossible.

If you go into the writing process knowing you will have to revise your work, you are more likely to be less inhibited. If you want to do an exercise to help you revise your work, try doing a blackout piece, where you blackout lines of your work.

PART V

EXPLORING POINT-OF-VIEW

41

FIRST PERSON

First person POV is about the narrator talking to a passive reader. The narrator may or may not be the protagonist of the story, and the narrator might be more than one person (possibly a group of people, like the town in William Faulkner's "A Rose for Emily").

First person stories use first person pronouns (I, me, we, us) when presenting the perspective of the narrator(s). There is an intimate feeling that comes from using this POV.

There are two things to watch out for, though: limitation of perspective, both physical and mental, and the trustworthiness of the narrator.

42

USING FIRST PERSON PLURAL

While this is not the most common usage of first person POV, it is an effective technique when used properly. I mentioned Faulkner's "A Rose for Emily" in the previous chapter. Its first sentence tips us off to the fact the story is being told from the collective first person POV of the town, more specifically its white men (which you can deduce from the way in which women are described). Another interesting tidbit is Black people are given different labels, depending on their proximity to affluent white people.

You can do these types of things with plural first person.

43

SECOND PERSON

Second person POV employs the use of second person pronouns (you, your) and typically requires the reader of the story be an active participant in the story.

There are two ways in which second person POV can be done. The first is making the reader the recipient of the actions of the narrator. This will look a lot like first person POV, but the reader (you) is directly involved in the story. It's like when you use the implied you for an instruction like "Pick up the clothes." The second way is to make the reader into the story's protagonist.

44

SECOND PERSON WHEN YOUR READER IS ON THE RECEIVING END OF THE NARRATOR'S ACTIONS

This is probably the most confusing use of second person, so remember how the reader is used is critical to the POV. Having the reader on the receiving end of the narrator's actions forces the reader to have an intimate connection to the plot of the story. A good example of this is Iain Pears's *The Portrait*, where the reader is pulled into the narrator's quest for revenge on the reader.

This might be challenging to carry throughout a novel, but it is ripe for using in a drabble.

Consider how you might involve your reader in your narrator's quest.

45

SECOND PERSON WHEN THE READER IS YOUR PROTAGONIST

This is the most common usage of second person POV. By putting you (the reader) in the place of the protagonist, it creates a very intimate connection between the reader and the plot.

You wake up one morning and decide that you've had enough. You will no longer stand for your neighbor allowing his dog to defecate on your lawn each morning.

All of the motivations, actions, and reactions of the character are directly tied to the reader. This intimate connection between the reader and the story enhances things in a way that other POVs may be unable to do.

46

THIRD PERSON OMNISCIENT

I sometimes refer to this as the "God-like" perspective, as omniscient literally means "all knowing." The trick with this type of third person POV is that you have to be careful about how much you actually share with the reader at any given moment. In other words, just because you can doesn't mean that you should. Ideally, you'd want to still allow for some mystery or unanswered questions, even if you have them all.

A good example of stories using third person omniscient is fairytales. They often share internal thoughts of characters, history, setting, and even scope of the story.

THIRD PERSON LIMITED

This POV allows the reader to see into the head of a single character, whether it be throughout an entire work or a section of that work. Here, the reader gets to follow the thoughts of the protagonist as she moves through the obstacles that challenge her.

This is similar to a singular first person POV, but it does not come with the weight of limitation of perspective and trustworthiness issues. It also, of course, uses third person pronouns instead of first person pronouns.

This is the most popular third person POV and is a rather safe choice to use.

48

THIRD PERSON DRAMATIC

Third person dramatic is different from omniscient and limited in that everything you learn about your characters is from what they say and what they do. Oftentimes those two things don't align, providing greater depth of character. (Imagine a character saying, "I love you" to another character but refusing to look that character in the eyes.)

One easy way of thinking about it is to see your story like a play or film. When we observe these characters, we learn of their motivations only by watching what they say and do.

While this may be challenging, it can be rewarding.

WHETHER YOU SHOULD MIX POINTS-OF VIEW

The short answer: no.

There are a number of novels out there that switch from first person to third person limited and back. I have even read stories, like Ambrose Bierce's "An Occurrence at Owl Creek Bridge," where all three third person POVs are used, in addition to both past and present tenses. With one hundred words, though, you don't have the space to be that experimental with POV.

When a reader begins to read a drabble, she must orient herself to the story quickly. Dabbling with different POVs can unmoor the story completely, making it difficult to establish consistency.

50

TRYING OUT VARIOUS POINTS-OF-VIEW

J ust because I discourage you from mixing POVs
doesn't mean that I feel you should limit yourself to writing with only one. Be agnostic with
your POVs. Use first person sometimes and third
person dramatic sometimes. Explore ways of using
second person. Be open to experimental approaches
to telling stories.

One of the key benefits of playing around with
POV choices is that you are using only one hundred
words to tell your story. Your commitment to a particular POV need extend no farther than that word
count.

Sometimes a story can be spiced up by using an
unexpected POV.

PART VI

DEVELOPING CHARACTERS

51

DEFINING WHAT A CHARACTER IS

I once read that a character is simply the representation of a human being. This definition considers the plethora of stories with animals as protagonists, as well as stories involving personification and anthropomorphism. The key to this definition is to understand that how we think about our character is directly related to how we see ourselves.

Your protagonist, as well as any other key characters in your story, should have a motivation, something driving him to seek a particular goal or outcome. The more we understand about our characters, the more realistic those characters' words and actions will be throughout.

52

ON PROTAGONISTS

The protagonist is the main character in a story. This character usually goes through obstacles testing her motivation. Her confronting of these obstacles will test her motivation, and this, overall, will give rise to what will become the plot of the story.

We tend to think of the protagonist as the *good guy*, but it might be best to think of the protagonist as the main character instead. Thanks to books where protagonists can have questionable ethics, even despicable behavior sometimes, laying off the "good guy" description will give you a greater blank slate on which to build your character.

53

ON ANTAGONISTS

Just like it is best to avoid using "good guy" language, it is also best to avoid using "bad guy" language. Rather, think of the antagonist as the character whose motivation runs counter to the protagonist's motivation. The reality is that, in most cases, each role is a matter of whose story you are choosing to tell.

Will there be circumstances in which your antagonist is evil? Maybe. But even the best antagonists have backstories that rival the protagonist's. Consider Erik "Killmonger" Stevens from *Black Panther* or Darth Vader from the *Star Wars* films.

Antagonists are as important as protagonists.

ROUND CHARACTERS VS. FLAT CHARACTERS

Round characters are dynamic by nature, which means they undergo changes. The way they behave at the beginning of the story and the way they behave at the end are different, whether that is a mild difference or a major one.

Flat characters, on the other hand, are static, which means they don't really change or evolve. Oftentimes, flat character protagonists will be paired with round characters as they go through obstacles together. You can see this in John Steinbeck's *Of Mice and Men* and in Winston Groom's *Forrest Gump*.

Interestingly, most protagonists in fiction (particularly microfiction) are round characters.

USING ARCHETYPES

An archetype is a character model oftentimes easily recognizable by the masses. At one point in time, archetypes were original character constructs, but since then they have evolved into something far more ubiquitous.

An example of an archetype is the "final girl" from horror movies. This is the last woman standing at the end of the story or film (*Halloween*, *Barbarian*, *Alien*, and *Scream*).

Should you use them? Well, that depends. The key to making sure your character is not a stereotype is to provide a realistic motivation. Make your character believable and readers just might cut you some slack.

56

AVOIDING PITFALLS WHEN WRITING ARCHETYPES

Sometimes when we use archetypes we can slide into stereotypes or overused tropes about these characters. No one wants to read a story they feel they have already read before. The key is to find a way to make your character more interesting, even if you are using an archetype.

Think about your character as a unique person with his own likes and dislikes, motivations, fears, loves, and livelihood. If you keep these things in the front of your mind, you will not yield to low hanging fruit when it comes to writing your characters. Your reader will thank you.

57

LOOK FOR INTERESTING CHARACTERS

Sometimes the character we envision as the protagonist is the least interesting character in the scene. I'm sure we have all seen television shows where the side characters are far more interesting than the protagonist. With a 100-word story, we should try to sidestep this situation. We simply do not have the word count or luxury of focusing on the least interesting person in the scene.

As an exercise, consider telling the story using other characters as the protagonist. Think more about how to engage your reader, as opposed to making them suffer through a milquetoast character's lackluster narrative journey.

58

INHABIT EVERY CHARACTER IN YOUR STORY

Oftentimes we spend so much time trying to perfect the protagonist that we neglect the other characters in the story. Ideally, we should pay attention to the motivations and needs of those characters as well. If we don't, they wind up becoming wallpaper characters or, in video game parlance, NPCs (non-playable characters).

If you thought enough to include the character in your drabble, there must be a reason for it. This harkens us back to the iceberg situation, where you know more about the character than you show. But trust me: the reader will know if your character is inauthentic.

59

LIMIT THE NUMBER OF
CHARACTERS YOU USE

When you approach a drabble, think of it like you're shooting a short film and you have a limited budget. Do you want to pay people to stand around, people who don't have a need to be in the scene? Probably not.

Well, in a drabble, your words are you currency. You only have 100 of them, so make each of them count.

To that end, you'll want to limit the number of characters you use. If you go over three characters, you should have a good reason. Most stories could thrive on three characters or fewer. Focus is important.

60

WRITING ABOUT CHARACTERS
WHO ARE DIFFERENT FROM YOU

If you decide to write about a character different from yourself, always lead with the character's humanity, not his race, impairment, gender identity, sexual orientation, religion, or age. If you belong to that community, you can do what you would normally do, but if you are from outside that community, be diligent in avoiding stereotypes, clunky descriptions, or things that might come across as insensitive or present a gaze that either fetishizes or eroticizes an "otherness" about the character. Leading with humanity means you're at least starting solidly.

Use sensitivity readers, if you have concerns (and even if you don't).

PART VII

EXPERIMENTING WITH YOUR WRITING

61

DICTIONARY REDUX

As writers, we should be in a constant state of improving our vocabularies. It doesn't have to be all homework, though. A quick idea for a story is to look up unusual words, be they archaic, arcane, or neologistic. You could easily write a story using the word, but why not go a step farther: create a fictional definition for the word with your own example of the word being used in a sentence. To raise the stakes a bit more, find a way to make the definition ironic or humorous in some way to imply a more complex story.

62

A RECEIPT

Admittedly, there are writers out there who are much better at this than I am. I have only written one of these successfully. All the same, it is a nonconventional approach to writing a drabble.

Think of a list of items that would appear on a store receipt. Consider what the items imply and what the totality of them suggests. Your story is being told between the lines

For example, a list of items one would use to construct an engagement ring might lend itself to a story. The key is to create a puzzle the reader will enjoy solving.

63

A RECIPE

Just like the receipt, you could use a recipe to imply a much larger story. People have a variety of relationships with foods, and within those relationships are a variety of stories.

Even better, consider a recipe you have seen in which the ingredients are not only unusual, but also hint at things that would suggest conflict or possibly the reaction to a point of tension within the story. Food also functions in many ways as a metaphor.

An added bonus is that most recipes are written in second person, which gives you a chance to flex those POV muscles.

64

A LETTER

Another good use of second person POV is to write an epistolary story. This simply means that your story is a letter to someone. Consider who would write the letter and to whom that character would send it. Why write this letter now? Why send it now? How will this letter affect the sender? How will it affect the receiver? With this type of story, you can suggest much of what would have happened before the letter was written, allowing you to use the "character response to the climax" technique as a way of entering the letter in medias res.

65

A FOOTNOTE

I magine an article from a peer-reviewed academic journal. It probably contains quite a few citations. Why not create a fake excerpt from an academic paper, inclusive of footnotes? With these footnotes, you could tell an entirely separate story from the one that is in the main text. This technique allows you to create a parallel situation in which the conflict is heightened due to the layers of storytelling you employ.

I have played around with footnotes in a few stories and have found this technique to be fun. It allows the writer to create commentary, while simultaneously telling a story.

SECTION OF A LARGER WORK

Revisiting the idea of taking from a section of a larger work, sans the footnotes, you could create a story by showing just a fraction of a longer page. There are various ways in which you can do this: writing a highlighted passage, writing what could represent a torn sheet from a notebook, a portion of a receipt, a portion of a recipe. The key is to show the reader the puzzle piece and have him figure out what the larger puzzle must look like based upon the shape of the piece and its tabs. Focus on implying the whole.

67

A JOURNAL ENTRY

Similar to writing a letter, writing a journal entry has an epistolary element to it. When people journal, they sometimes write to the journal, to their future selves, or even curate their entries to speak to a specific person who might one day inherit their journal. Either way, journal entries bring about an interesting form of storytelling, especially when viewed through the lens of microfiction.

Figure out what day you are writing and the significance of that day. Like with any other drabble, you will want to consider what you are implying and what you want the reader to understand.

68

TELLING A STORY OUT OF ORDER

In 1994, I watched Quentin Tarantino's film *Pulp Fiction* for the first time. Once I finished the film, I immediately began reorganizing the film in my head into a chronological narrative. Since then, I have seen number of films and read a number of books where the stories are told out of sequence.

With a drabble, there is limited space to tell things out of order, but if you are crafty, you can find a way to shift your narrative in an unexpected way for your reader. Understanding your story gives you the liberty of being inventive with its structure.

TELLING A META STORY

Meta simply means that the story refers to itself or is, in some way, self-aware. If I am writing a story about myself writing a story, this is an example of a meta story.

Perhaps you have seen horror films that are aware (in some way) that they are horror films (like *Scream* or *Cabin in the Woods*). Perhaps you write a story in which your protagonist realizes she is a character in a story you are writing (like *Stranger Than Fiction*). All of these ideas are meta stories.

This story can be entertaining, but try to avoid overusing it.

70

WRITING A REVIEW OF A
FICTIONAL STORY

When I lived in New York, back in the late 90s, I enjoyed reading film reviews by Janet Maslin of the *New York Times*. Over the years, I have come to appreciate the value of a well-written review.

For me, I decided to apply this strategy to writing stories, except rather than write a story about a person reviewing a work, I opted to make the story the review of an imaginary work.

This type of story implies the original artwork at its center, as well as its juxtaposition to other fictional or real work, in a professional way.

PART VIII

EDITING

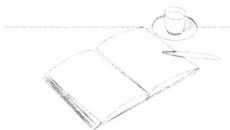

71

WHY EDITING IS IMPORTANT?

Editing is important. There's no way around it.

First drafts are written with great enthusiasm and commitment to getting the story onto the page. The part of our brain at work is the creative side, not the analytical side. In the film *Finding Forrester*, William Forrester (played by Sean Connery) comments to his protégé, Jamal, that he should write the first draft with his heart and the second draft with his head.

Editing is the necessary component of applying your analytical mind to your draft in an effort to tighten, correct, and even improve the final version of your work.

72

BECOMING COMFORTABLE WITH EDITING

There are a lot of writers who are quick to say that editing should be the job of someone else. They prefer to focus strictly on the creative part of things, but to relinquish a solid understanding of editing, as well as grammar and mechanics, to another person is like a mechanic expecting someone else to know what tool he should be using when repairing a car.

This is not to say editors are not important, but when you write microfiction, there is no way around knowing where a comma should go or whether a sentence contains a dangling modifier.

CONTENT EDITING

Content editing is about making sure your content is consistent. If the dress is purple on page 12, it should not magically become red on page 23 (unless that is a plot element). Many times we are writing so quickly that was don't notice that we spelled a name one way on one page and a different way on another.

Because drabbles are so short, this is unlikely to be an error, but in keeping with our desire to write something publishable, we should not take any chances with continuity throughout the text. This is something we can do ourselves.

74

LINE EDITING

L ine editing is about making sure you are using the right number of words to convey your idea. Consider the following sentences:

Cheryl laughed so hard everyone could hear her on the other side of the room.

Cheryl's laughter echoed across the room.

You will notice the second sentence is more succinct, not that there is anything wrong with the first sentence. Line editing just makes the sentence sharper and cleaner.

When you are able to trim unnecessary words, it frees you up to replace those cut words with other words that might bring greater resonance to your overall story.

75

COPY EDITING

With fiction, copy editing is largely about making sure spelling, grammar, punctuation, and other mechanical errors in the work have been satisfactorily addressed. And yes, there are people who do this job professionally. However, since you are writing stories of no more than 100 words, it would be a good idea to teach yourself to understand and apply these rules to your own work.

In my classes, I oftentimes pose this question to my students: if you cannot write a sentence correctly, why would anyone want to read your entire story?

We owe it to ourselves to understand copy editing.

76

GRAMMAR, PART 1

The first thing to teach yourself about grammar is subject/verb agreement. There are plenty of good books on this subject. First and foremost, you have to allow yourself to understand there are things you can still learn, despite your having spoken English most of your life.

Learn the rules regarding indefinite pronouns and collective nouns, too. Learn to identify the subject cleanly and make the verb and any pronoun antecedent agree in number.

Consider this sentence:

Each of the girls plays on her iPhone before falling asleep.

Because of how we speak, this sounds wrong. But it is correct.

77

GRAMMAR, PART 2

Another area of grammar that tends to confuse people is modifiers, more specifically dangling and misplaced modifiers. The reason we have modifier rules is so people don't get confused about what we are actually trying to communicate.

With dangling modifiers, the independent clause and opening subordinate clause don't link up. Consider the error in this sentence:

Before washing the clothes, the bed was made.

With misplaced modifiers, what is being modified must be next to its modifier, not placed somewhere else in the sentence. Consider the error in this sentence:

I am taking a course next semester on Toni Morrison.

MECHANICS, PART 1

Punctuation is critical, especially in small works. A comma splice, improperly used colon, missing or additional comma, awkwardly used semicolon, or some odd usage of punctuation can throw the presentation of a story into doubt and have a more discerning reader shake her head, wondering if you cared too little about mechanics to get these things right.

In grade school, many of us received shortcuts and pseudo-rules for how to punctuate a sentence. I strongly encourage you to look up the rules for using these punctuation marks. Don't assume you know everything just because nobody has ever corrected you before.

79

MECHANICS, PART 2

S pelling is important, which is yet another reason to keep a dictionary close by. Even more, it is important to understand the concept of homonyms (words with the same name), homophones (words that sound the same but are spelled differently), and homographs (words that are spelled the same but pronounced differently). Oftentimes, words that are misspelled are homophone errors, like "emigrate" and "immigrate" or "to" and "too."

Then there are errors that have gradually become more acceptable, like writing "alright" instead of "all right." This does not carry over to "a lot" (which is and has always been two words).

80

THE IMPORTANCE OF A SECOND SET OF EYES

No matter how many times you read your work, before editing it and after editing it, it is important to get a trusted second set of eyes to read your story before you send it out.

Our eyes have a funny way of playing tricks on us. Once we have allowed our brains to fill in omissions or to see past errors, we need someone completed disconnected from the work to do a cold reading. The reality is when we read, we don't always catch every improper word, punctuation, or misspelling.

Do your best. Then have someone else read it.

PART IX

PUBLISHING YOUR 100-WORD STORIES

HOW TO KNOW WHEN YOUR STORY IS READY

This is like asking a visual artist when does she know her painting is finished. There are several ways to know when the story is ready.

1. You have an innate understanding that there is nothing further you can do to the story.

2. You give yourself permission to stop tinkering with it.

3. You feel that you have done the best you can with it.

4. You say, "To hell with it," and move on.

It's all subjective. It's like Supreme Court Justice Potter Stewart attempting to define pornography: you'll just have to know it when you see it.

LITERARY JOURNALS

One of the first places you should look to submit your work is a literary journal, either print or electronic. In the past few years a number of journals have become popular among microfictionists. For 100-word story writers in particular, the first place to check out is *100 Word Story*, the grandfather of journals devoted to this form. Also, check out *The Centifictionist*, *The Drabble*, and *A Story in 100 Words*. These deal exclusively with 100-word stories. There are also a number of journals devoted to microfiction, exclusive of word count, like *Smokelong Quarterly*, and journals devoted to flash fiction.

83

ANTHOLOGIES

I f you want your drabble to appear in an actual book, then you will want to consider submitting to one of the anthologies out there devoted to microfiction. Because of the nature of anthologies, you have to be diligent to find out when they are seeking submissions.

Some anthologies are compiled by literary journals seeking to highlight their "greatest hits," while other have an editing team looking to build a collection of new work around a particular theme.

To find out a list of current anthologies seeking microfiction submissions, it would be helpful to subscribe to a site like Duotrope.

84

COMPETITIONS

Maybe you are not yet ready to submit your work to a literary journal or an anthology and you are still trying to figure out if you have any skill at writing a drabble. If that is the case, consider submitting your work to a competition. (Understand that there are very skilled writers also submitting their works here, as well, so it won't be a free pass by a long shot.) Still, it is good to see how you fare with other writers of the form, assuming you care about that. Just be aware some competitions will charge a fee.

85

KEEPING TRACK OF SUBMISSIONS

Y ou should not submit to one place and sit back and wait to hear from them before you begin working on new stories. It can sometimes take as long as six months to hear back from a publisher, although most will respond much sooner. You should always be writing new stories and sending them out.

Because of the flurry of activity you will likely create, you will want to create a spreadsheet that, at minimum, lists the journal or anthology or contest, the date you submitted, the type of submission, and the title of the work. Aim to stay organized.

86

PUBLISHING YOUR WORK ON YOUR WEBSITE

Because of the novelty of writing drabbles, sometimes a writer might prefer to simply publish his stories on his own website, blog, Substack, or mailing list. These are perfectly fine.

Publishing your work in this way allows people who already follow you to give you feedback on your work, which allows for a more immediate form of gratification (if you will).

If you elect to do this, however, please understand that you are *publishing* your work, which might bar it from being accepted by other journals or anthologies, as most publishers want original, unpublished work and the first serial rights.

87

PUBLISHING YOUR WORK ON
SOCIAL MEDIA

Some writers decide to publish their drabbles on social media sites, eschewing the print form, while others may prefer an audiovisual format. Doing this could have the same benefits I mentioned in the previous chapter, as well as the same overall concerns. The key is to decide what you want to do with the story.

Personally, I don't put my work on social media, as I tend to look for places to publish it in ways that will either help build and enhance my brand or lead to me getting paid for my work.

Decide what is best for you.

88

COMPILING YOUR BEST STORIES
INTO A COLLECTION

Whether or not you seek publication for your individual stories, once you feel you have enough good drabbles for a book, you can began to build your own collection.

What constitutes *enough*? That depends on a number of factors. Are you submitting your collection to a publisher or self-publishing? Will your book appear in print or electronic form only? The production requirements are different for each. For example, if you have a print book, you will want to make sure you have enough pages so your book has a spine (perfect binding), as opposed to saddle stitched (with staples).

SUBMITTING TO PUBLISHERS

One of the harsh realities surrounding publishing books of microfiction is that there are not a lot of publishers out there seeking this kind of work. While there are some here and there, the number of publishers seeking more traditional book content is exponentially more.

If you are interested in going this route, I would urge you to check the names of the publishers of the microfiction collections you own (yes, you should be financially supporting your microfiction community). If the publisher is a larger one, check the Acknowledgment section for an agent's name, then consider querying your work there.

90

PUBLISHING YOUR OWN
COLLECTION

S elf-publishing is not easy. There are many hats you have to wear, including editing, layout, production, printing, marketing, and promoting. Many of these things can be outsourced (or you could develop the skills to do everything). Still, going this route can be extremely rewarding (and in all honesty, you could possibly earn more money this way).

For microfiction, this may be one of the more likely ways to make it into print, given the sales of microfiction collections are not usually at the level of traditionally published novels.

If you go this route, please be patient and manage your expectations.

PART X

PARTING THOUGHTS

BECOME A JACK OF ALL TRADES
AND A MASTER OF THEM ALL

B ecause you are working with a short form, it would be ideal if you could take the time to learn to do clean edits of your own work. You could also learn how to publish and distribute your work. Many authors have successfully managed these tasks.

When I first started, I took each summer to learn and refine a new skill set. If you develop these skills now, when you become more prolific, the machine for getting your work into the world will be much more oiled and ready to produce art.

It is *not* impossible to do it all.

92

TRY TO AVOID DELEGATING
THINGS YOU CAN LEARN TO DO

Everything you delegate to someone else is a potential expense you will incur with your work. This is not to say there is no value in hiring others to handle more challenging tasks, but you have to be honest with yourself: microfiction is not the most lucrative area of publishing, so there might be greater challenges in recouping upfront costs.

If you teach yourself to edit well, you might be able to get by with a beta reader or two. Ideally, when it comes to publishing, the money should flow towards you as much as possible, as opposed to away.

READ AS MUCH AS YOU CAN

As I mentioned earlier in this book, to get good at writing 100-word stories, you should strongly consider reading them daily. You should indulge in as many 100-word stories as you can.

You will learn a great deal from consuming a lot of art. For one, you will learn what is good and what is not so good. You will find yourself in awe of what one writer can do with the form and find yourself thinking surely you could write a better 100-word story than another writer. Both are forms of motivation. Live and breathe 100-word stories each day.

94

DON'T WORRY ABOUT GENRE

E ven though you may come across anthologies that are entirely horror or entirely science fiction, I encourage you to be agnostic with regard to genres. The simple act of crafting a good drabble already establishes the form itself as a genre.

This frees you up to experiment with different types of stories. Even though you might be a romance writer, you might decide to write something more "literary" in nature. If you're a horror writer, you may be tempted to write a western story. The sky is the limit when it comes to subject matter. Allow yourself to be free.

SUPPORT OTHER WRITERS OF 100-WORD STORIES

Previously, I mentioned that you should read as many 100-word stories as you can, whether they be in print or online. You should also buy collections of 100-word stories by a single author. As you have probably discovered, it takes a tremendous amount of effort to write a single story, so when a person has written enough good ones to form a book, we should, at least, read a sample of it, if not buy it or request our local library purchase a copy for its collection. It never hurts to be a good literary citizen of the microfiction community.

96

SHARE THE CONCEPT OF 100-WORD STORIES WITH OTHERS

I f you have cared enough to read this far into the book, you are clearly interested in both writing, reading, and supporting the microfiction community. Now here's the fun part: take your enthusiasm for the form and share it with everyone you know who might find this form fascinating.

Since I began writing microfiction, I have spoken at conferences, worked with libraries, incorporated exercises into my university teaching, written articles, and spoken on podcasts. I am not asking you to do all of those things, but if you talk with others about the form, it can go a long way.

HAVE REALISTIC EXPECTATIONS ABOUT THE POPULARITY OF 100-WORD STORIES

Because there is still much evangelizing on 100-word stories to be done, understand there are plenty of people out there who have never heard of them, most of whom will think this is a passing fad or that it is impossible to write anything good in so few words. Because of this, they will approach buying or reading a collection of drabbles with some degree of skepticism. Consequently, you are unlikely to sell enough books or stories to quit your day job. Perhaps that will change in the future, but understand the form, as of today, is far from popular.

APPLYING 100-WORD STORY
TECHNIQUES TO LONGER WORKS

Some people write microfiction as a way of sharpening their storytelling skills between longer projects. There are several benefits to doing this, not the least of which is that it helps you to strengthen your scenes so that you are still telling a story, even when you are exploring the minutiae of that scene. Some writers make each paragraph of their novel sing by remembering the importance of a single paragraph. Each sentence should make you want to read more—explore more—and writing 100-word stories helps to develop the skill set necessary to take complete advantage of each scene.

TRAIN YOURSELF TO WRITE
WITHOUT A MUSE

Because drabbles are often the length of short poems, it is easy to think you must wait for a muse to arrive so that you can write something. I discourage you from doing this. In fiction writing, much of getting your writing done is by sitting down and doing the work. In the end, few, if any, will know which of your stories was born of inspiration versus which ones came from sitting still and writing. In the end, the more drabbles you write, the better you will be able to write them. Train yourself to not need a muse.

100

KEEP WRITING AND PUSHING YOURSELF

I try not to get too comfortable with what and how I write. Writing should be an adventure, and the goal is to keep moving forward, learning new things, and pushing yourself to explore writing in different ways. When I first began writing, I wrote novels. Now I write microfiction primarily. To me, there are so many things I have yet to learn.

Writing this book is a way of pushing myself to do more, and I hope this book has helped you to want to do more.

Writing is a gift. Always seek to make the most of it.

RECOMMENDED READINGS

Bible, James. *Dead Mech*. Jake Bible Fiction LLC, 2019.

Culbertson, Kim, and Grant Faulkner. *100-Word Stories: A Short Form for Expansive Writing*. Heinemann, 2023.

Drayton, Erica. *The First 100: 100-Word Stories*. Pd Books, 2024.

Drayton, Erica. *The Second 100: 100-Word Stories*. Pd Books, 2024.

Drayton, Erica. *The Third 100: 100-Word Stories*. Pd Books, 2024.

Drayton, Erica. *The Fourth 100: 100-Word Stories*. Pd Books, 2024.

Faulkner, Grant. *Fissures: One Hundred 100-Word Stories*. Press 53, 2017.

Faulkner, Grant, et al. *Nothing Short Of: Selected Tales from* 100 Word Story. Outpost19, 2018.

Jones, Daniel, and Miya Lee. *Tiny Love Stories: True Tales of Love in 100-Words or Less*. Artisan, 2020.

Kennedy, M. L. *100 by 100: Stories in 100 Words*. Rock 'n' Roll Dino, 2016.

Loomis, K. Kris. *100 Tiny Tales: Short Stories Told in Exactly One Hundred Words*. Lililoom Publishing, 2019.

Massa, Kyla A. *Hecatontagonal Stew: A Collection of 100 Hundred-Word Stories*, 2024.

Scotellaro, Robert. *Bad Motel: 100-Word Stories*. Big Table Publishing Company, 2016.

Smidts, Michael E. *One Hundred Words: A Collection of Short Stories*. Storeylines Press, 2023.

Strohm, Paul. *Sportin' Jack*. CreateSpace Independent Publishing Platform, 2012.

Walker, Ran. *Black Marker: A Novel in 100-Word Stories*. Black and Square, 2022.

Walker, Ran. *A Burst of Gray: A Novel in 100-Word Stories*. 45 Alternate Press, LLC, 2021.

Walker, Ran. *A Different Kind of Christmas Story: A Carol in 100-Word Stories*. 45 Alternate Press, LLC, 2022.

Walker, Ran. *Four Suits: A Deck of 100-Word Stories*. Black and Square, 2024.

Walker, Ran. *GloKat and the Art of Timing: A Novel in 100-Word Stories*. Worldspark Studios, 2022.

Walker, Ran. *Keep It 100: 100-Word Stories*. 45 Alternate Press, LLC, 2021.

Walker, Ran. *The Library of Afro Curiosities: 100-Word Stories*. 45 Alternate Press, LLC, 2022.

Walker, Ran. *Parts of Speech: 100-Word Stories*. Black and Square, 2023.

Walker, Ran. *This Is Not a Poem/Story: 100-Word Stories*. Black and Square, 2023.

*Note: This is by no means an exhaustive list, but it will get you started.

ACKNOWLEDGMENTS
IN 100 WORDS

Thank you to my beautiful wife and wonderful daughter, my parents, my brother and his family, my wife's family, my fellow writers, my colleagues, my students, and those who have read and supported me over the years on this strange and interesting creative journey.

Special thanks to Grant Faulkner, Paul Strohm, Kim Culbertson, Clara Ray Rusinek Klein, Lynn Mundell, Gayle Towell, Beret Olson, and all of the people who have helped to elevate this particular form.

Finally, thanks to Quincy Jones (RIP) and James Ingram (RIP) for the song that inspired the title of this book.

I appreciate you all.

ABOUT THE AUTHOR

IN 100 WORDS

Ran Walker (he/him) is the author of over 35 books. His short stories, flash fiction, microfiction, and poetry have appeared in a variety of anthologies and journals.

He is the winner of the Indie Author Project's National Indie Author of the Year Award, the Black Caucus of the American Library Association Best Fiction Ebook Award, the Virginia Indie Author Project Award for Adult Fiction, and the Blind Corner Afrofuturism Microfiction Contest. Ran is an Associate Professor of English and Creative Writing at Hampton University and teaches with Writer's Digest University. He lives in Virginia with his wife and daughter.

ALSO BY RAN WALKER

A Burst of Gray: A Novel In 100-Word Stories

The Library of Afro Curiosities: 100-Word Stories

Black Marker: A Novel in 100-Word Stories

GloKat and the Art of Timing: A Novel in 100-Word Stories

A Different Kind of Christmas Story: A Carol in 100-Word Stories

Spaceships Don't Come Equipped with Rearview Mirrors: 50-Word Stories

This Is Not a Poem/Story: 100-Word Stories

Parts of Speech: 100-Word Stories

Four Suits: A Deck of 100-Word Stories

O'ahu: Prose Poems

Apollo's Toy Box

Gods Among Men

One Hundred Ways: A Handbook for Writing 100-Word Stories

www.ingramcontent.com/pod-product-compliance
Lightning Source LLC
Chambersburg PA
CBHW052021030426
42335CB00026B/3239